# The Little Book of Playground Games

Simple games

by Simon M̶ ̶.̶.̶.̶.̶̶.̶̶̶

Additional Material by Sally Featherstone

Illustrations by Martha Hardy

## LITTLE BOOKS WITH **BIG** IDEAS

Published 2010 by A&C Black Publishers Limited
36 Soho Square, London W1D 3QY
www.acblack.com

ISBN 978-1-9041-8789-9

First published in the UK 2004 by Featherstone Education

Text © Simon MacDonald, 2004
Series Editor, Sally Featherstone
Illustrations © Martha Hardy, 2004
Cover photographs © Shutterstock

Printed in Great Britain by Latimer Trend & Company Limited

This book is produced using paper that is made from wood grown in
managed, sustainable forests. It is natural, renewable and recyclable.

The logging and manufacturing processes conform to the environmental
regulations of the country of origin.

**To see our full range of titles
visit www.acblack.com**

# Contents

# Introduction

The playing of games is something that comes naturally to us all. Games teach many of the social skills necessary for a balanced, effective and productive life. Through games we learn how to share, take turns, exult in our own and others' successes as well as applaud the efforts of our friends and peers.

Rules provide the framework for us to assimilate the moral values expected of us as responsible citizens in society – games and game playing should never be underestimated! Games underpin the entire teaching and learning process.

This book aims to provide a resource for practitioners, teaching assistants, playgroup workers; in fact, anyone enthusiastic about the fantastic contribution that games play in the development of self-esteem, group work, concentration and attention, and, most of all, sharing.

## Why play games?

There is an interesting and emotive debate concerning the 'winning' and 'losing' aspect of competitive games. Most people would accept that there is a competitive edge to games and sports that has to be acknowledged. What is beneficial is the fact that children can measure their previous achievement with their new best effort, and at the same time strive to improve their skills.

However, the negative aspect of competition in games can be that some children do not feel valued and cannot compete with friends and peers to the same level. These children become discouraged and their negative feelings about themselves are compounded. They become less involved in games and by the time they reach Year 1, they dread playground activities, as something to endure rather than enjoy.

The remedy for this is to make a concerted effort to reintroduce old games, which are often more social and verbally interactive, while encouraging the trying out of newer ones. It has to be supported by the whole setting community and the good habits it instills in our Early Years Foundation Stage children will have endless benefits as they move along the Key Stages.

## Getting Started

The successful introduction of a games-playing ethos relies on the involvement and support of all the children and adults who work and play at each setting.

When considering the systematic introduction of games, get the views and opinions of all the adults who work with children out of doors.

These may include:

▶ teachers and other practitioners in nurseries and

▶ reception classes

▶ dining supervisors

▶ after school staff

▶ parent and student helpers

They will give you valuable information about the games and activities that are already popular with the children. You will also find out where the problems are and which activities give most cause for concern.

Then ask the children what they like and dislike about being outside. Do they have favourite games that they would like to play?

Perhaps there could be time made for them to be a 'games expert' and teach their friends their favourite activity. P.E. sessions are also good times to teach new games that can be expanded upon in the outdoor sessions. The setting could have a 'game of the week' that everyone has a go at.

Don't forget that parents and carers are an immensely rich source of knowledge and skills. Include them in your fact-finding. They may be able to bring new games or variants that will prove very popular with all.

# Tips for setting up

During the game playing times, the following may be of help when facing the common problems of choosing individuals and of picking teams. You will already have many strategies of your own, but these seem to work well.

1. Teams can be chosen randomly. If two teams are needed, children can be numbered as 1, 2, 1, 2, etc.

2. Teams can be chosen by hair colour or the predominant colours they are wearing.

3. Birthdays can be a useful method of splitting a group in half – January to June on one side and July to December on the other.

4. Pass an object around the circle. When the person leading the game turns away, they call out 'IT!' and the person left holding the object is 'IT'. Alternatively, you could sing the following song as the object is passed from child to child:

   'Pass around the magic hat/feather/shell, magic hat, magic hat,
   Pass around the magic hat, who will play our game?'

   Whoever is left holding the object on the last word of the song is now 'IT'.

5. With older children, you could put lots of pieces of paper in a hat, one of which is marked 'IT' and allow each player to draw a piece from it.

## What sort of games could we play?

In this book you will find a range of different sorts of games:

▶ Name Games
   – which help children to take turns, realise their uniqueness, listen carefully and experience a chance to be special.

▶ Energisers
   – which will get children going at the beginning of a session, or let off steam in bad weather.

▶ Traditional Games
   – to remind you of some of the games you may have played when you were at school.

▶ Circle Games
   – to play indoors or out, in all weathers.

▶ Games from around the World
   – international versions of games you may know by different names.

▶ New Games
   – some new twists on old favourites, or ones you may not know.

▶ Co-operative Games
   – including some parachute play.

▶ Singing games
   – traditional singing games which need to be preserved, mainly because children enjoy them so much!

Most of the games can be played by children of all ages.

# Links with the Early Years Foundation Stage Goals

The following are projected goals for children at the end of Early Years Foundation Stage. They have been selected as being particularly relevant to game playing.

## Personal, Social and Emotional Development

▶ Continue to be interested, excited and motivated to learn

▶ Be confident to try new activities and speak in a familiar group

▶ Maintain attention, concentration and sit quietly when appropriate

▶ Form good relationships with adults and peers; work as part of a group, taking turns and sharing fairly, understanding that there need to be agreed values and codes of behaviour

## Communication, language and literacy

▶ Interact with others and take turns

▶ Sustain attentive listening, responding to what they have heard by relevant comments, questions or actions

▶ Speak clearly and audibly with confidence

▶ Use language to imagine and recreate roles and experiences

## Physical development

▶ Move with confidence, imagination and in safety

▶ Move with control and co-ordination

▶ Show awareness of space, of themselves and others

## Creative development

▶ Use their imagination in creative activities

▶ Express and communicate their ideas, thoughts and feelings

# Name and pass

**Group size:** any
**Age:** any
**Equipment:** a large, soft ball

In this game, the player with the ball has to say the name of another player and roll the ball to them. It is important that everyone remembers to say the name first before they send the object as it alerts the receiver to what happens next! Two-part instructions are good practice for young children.

## How to play:

1. Sit down in a circle with a little space between each player.
2. Choose one player to start the game.
3. The child with the ball says the name of someone else in the circle and rolls the ball along the ground to them.
4. The receiver chooses another child to send the ball to, says their name and rolls the ball.
5. Continue until everyone has had a go.

## Variations:

▶ Start the game with all players standing up and throwing the ball. Players sit down when they have had a turn.

▶ Make the game more difficult as the children get better at it by making the ball smaller.

# What a look

**Group size:** any
**Age:** any
**Equipment:** none

This game is a variation on Name and pass, but a look is sent across the circle rather than a ball.

## How to play:

1. The players stand in a circle and one is chosen to start the game.

2. They decide who they will cross the circle to meet. They do this by looking at someone and making eye contact with them.

3. The child says the name of the other child and moves towards them.

4. While they are doing this, the other child makes eye contact with someone else across the circle and begins to move towards them.

5. The object of the game is to move before another player gets to your space.

6. It may be too difficult a task for very young children at first, so you could just encourage them to 'find a friend' – move and stand next to the person they have made eye contact with. The moving before they arrive could be introduced later.

## Variations:

▶ Play 'Look and roll' with a ball or 'Look and toss' with a bean bag.

▶ Play 'Look and shake hands' by looking at another player who gets up and meets you in the middle to shake hands.

# Catch it!

**Group size:** any
**Age:** any
**Equipment:** a bean bag and cones

This game is great fun and a really energetic way to start any games session, especially in cold weather.

## How to play:

1. Make a clearly defined space using cones or markers.

2. Tell the children that you want them to walk around the space keeping their eyes and ears open. Tell them that in a moment you are going to pass the beanbag to someone by calling their name and then throwing it to them. They must try to catch the beanbag and then pass it on to someone else in the same way.

3. Continue to pass the beanbag as you walk, until everyone has had a turn or you are all worn out! Emphasise the safety aspect of this game – always be looking out for each other and the beanbag.

## Variations:

▶ Change the way the children must travel – hopping, skipping, jumping, even walking backwards.

▶ Play 'Pretend catch it' – with an imaginary ball!

▶ As the children get older and used to the game, you could have two bean bags passing round at the same time – perhaps one for the boys and one for the girls.

# Simon says

**Group size:** any
**Age:** any
**Equipment:** none

This well known game is good for developing concentration. It's also a lot of fun. Games like this, which are instantly recognisable will always be popular and it is our job to continue to promote them for future generations of children.

## How to play:

1. Make a circle.
2. Choose a leader. With younger or inexperienced players, this should be an adult. Children can take over when you feel they are ready.
3. The leader performs a series of actions for the group to copy. Before each action the leader says (for example) 'Simon says...put your hands on your head.'
4. The players must copy the leader unless the leader leaves out the 'Simon says...' bit.
5. Give the children a few practice runs.
6. Then anyone who does make a mistake should fold their arms and sit down until the game is over.
7. It's essential that the game is played quickly. That way no one is left out for too long.

## Variations:

▶ Everyone except the leader shuts their eyes!

# Little pirates

**Group size:** any
**Age:** any
**Equipment:** some coloured
cones or tape, or coloured
chalk (two or more colours)

You may know this game as 'Take the
Ship'. The rules are very similar, and
have been simplified for very young
children. It is good for concentration
and is an excellent warm-up for a
continuing games session.

## How to play:

1. The children form a line down the middle of a clearly marked area.

2. Make two other lines about 3m away from this line on each side. Make these different colours!

3. Choose a leader who shouts the instructions: this should be an adult till the children know the game.
   'Go to Blue' – everyone runs to the blue line
   'Go to Red' – everyone runs to the red line
   'Go to the middle' – everyone runs back to the middle line

4. The leader shouts the orders faster and faster.

5. Continue until everyone is worn out!

## Variations:

▶ Play like sailors with 'Go to port', 'Go to starboard', 'Go to midships'.

▶ Add other instructions like: 'Salute the Captain', 'Scrub the deck', 'Climb the rigging', 'Look through your telescope'.

▶ Play so that the last person to respond to an instruction or makes a mistake is out. Play till no-one is left.

# What's the time Mr Wolf?

**Group size:** any
**Age:** any
**Equipment:** chalk

A traditional favourite that most children will already be familiar with. While most adults will remember playing it with Mr Wolf facing a wall, this isn't essential!

## How to play:

1. One child is 'Mr Wolf'. They face away from the rest of the children who form a group some distance away – on a line or in a chalk circle.

2. The children ask 'What's the time Mr Wolf?' He/she replies with 'five o'clock', 'one o'clock', etc.

3. Each time Mr Wolf replies, the children take that number of steps towards his back.

4. When Mr Wolf decides that it's 'Dinnertime!' he/she turns and runs towards the children who must try and get back to the starting place before Mr Wolf grabs them.

5. The first player to be caught becomes the next Mr Wolf.

## Variations:

▶ Move with hops, jumps or giant strides.
▶ Tie the ends of a rope together and use it for a 'home'. All the children must get inside and hold the rope up around them.

# Ring-a-roses

**Group size:** any
**Age:** any
**Equipment:** none

This popular circle game/chant dates back to the time of the Great Plague in England. It can be played with any number of children.

## How to play:

1. Make a circle with the children.

2. Say or sing:
   'Ring-a-ring of roses, a pocket full of posies',
   the children walk around in a circle holding hands.
   'Atishoo-atishoo',

   the children stop, bend their knees on each sneeze.
   and on 'We all fall down!' they fall to the floor.

3. Another verse was added later for those unhappy with the plague reference. It goes:
   Fishes in the water, (move like a fish on the floor)
   Fishes in the sea.
   We all jump up with a 1-2-3! (jump to your feet)

## Variations:

▶ Play the game several times in a row, getting faster and faster each time.

# Bingo

Group size: any
Age: any
Equipment: none

This is a popular song and an ideal chant/game to start a group session with very young children.

## How to play:

1. All the players stand in a circle and the song starts like this:
   'I knew a man who had a dog and Bingo was his name.
   B.I.N.G.O, B.I.N.G.O, B.I.N.G.O
   And Bingo was his name – O!'

2. The next time round, the first letter of Bingo is missed out and replaced with a clap instead.

3. Carry on until everyone just claps the name.

## Variations:

▶ Try missing off the last letter each time.

▶ Use other names or words instead of BINGO.

Remember, clapping games help learning by encouraging children to use both hands.

17

# Looby Lou

**Group size:** any
**Age:** any
**Equipment:** none

Another traditional song that many adults will remember!

## How to play:

1. The children find a partner and hold hands facing each other.

2. Start by swinging their joined hands up and down, then swinging round while you sing the chorus:

   'Here we go Looby Lou, here we go Looby Light,
   Here we go Looby Lou, all on a Saturday night'

3. Then sing:

   'Put your right hand in, your right hand out,
   In, out, in, out, shake it all about.
   Here we go Looby Lou, here we go Looby Light,
   Here we go Looby Lou, all on a Saturday night.'

3. Repeat the chorus between each verse, starting with your left hand, right hand, left foot, right foot, and finally your whole body!

## Variations:

▶ Add other body parts such as elbows, shoulders, ears, thumbs, knees, even eyebrows or heels.

# Stuck in the mud

**Group size:** large
**Age:** any
**Equipment:** none

A popular game with many variations, best played on grass if you can. It is suitable for large groups of children.

## How to play:

1. Get the children to spread themselves out in the marked space

2. Choose one child to be 'IT'.

3. On 'GO!' all the children run around in the space chased by 'IT'. If 'IT' manages to touch anyone, they must stand still with their arms outstretched at the sides and their legs apart in a starshape.

4. They remain like this until one of the other players crawls between their legs to release them. They can now rejoin the game.

5. The game continues until 'IT' is so exhausted that they cannot chase anymore or everyone has been tagged!

## Variations:

▶ Use a different shape to 'freeze' into.

▶ Children who are stuck in the mud must be freed by two other players touching them at the same time.

# Archway tag

**Group size:** an even number
**Age:** over five
**Equipment:** none

This is a variation on Stuck in the mud, and involves children in working in pairs. For this reason it is important to have an even number of players.

## How to play:

1. Each child finds a partner, someone they are happy to hold hands with.

2. One pair is then chosen to be 'ON'. They chase the other pairs and try to tag them.

3. If either one of a pair is touched then they must form an arch with their partner.

4. Other pairs can release them by running under the arch. They can then rejoin the game.

5. If any pair breaks hands while they are running, they also have to form an arch

6. If the pair who are 'ON' break hands, then all the pairs that they have caught are released.

7. Change the chasing pair as often as possible.

## Variations:

▶ Try the game in threes or fours for a variation for older children.

# Duck, duck, goose

**Group size:** any
**Age:** any
**Equipment:** none

A very popular circle game, full of suspense for the players! A whole class can play, although for younger children it may be better to split the group in half with an adult helping each group.

## How to play:

1. Sit down in a circle with a little space between each person.

1. One child is chosen to be IT. They walk around the outside of the circle and touch their hand gently (emphasise this!) on the head of each child they pass. They say 'Duck, duck, duck...' as they go.

1. They decide when to say 'Goose!' as they place their hand on the head of the next child.

1. Then both children run around the outside of the circle in opposite directions and try to get back to the empty space before the other. The last one back continues to walk around the circle as before saying 'Duck, duck, duck...' until they again choose 'Goose!'

## Variations:

▶ Hop, skip, jump round the circle.

▶ The 'Goose' chases the other player, going round the same way, until they get back to the space.

# Find the ring

**Group size:** any
**Age:** any
**Equipment:** a long piece of string or ribbon (big enough to go round the circle); a ring or hair scrunchie

This circle game is simple to play, and requires good observation and good pretending!

## How to play:

1. Sit down in a circle with a little space between each player.
2. Thread the ring or scrunchie on the string or ribbon and tie the ends of the ribbon or string together.
3. Choose someone to stand in the middle of the circle to be 'The Guesser.'
4. The children in the ring must pass the ring along the string, inside their hands, so the Guesser can't see who has the ring.
5. Count to ten or twenty as the children slide the ring along the string.
6. When you get to ten, the Guesser has to guess who has the ring.
7. If (or when) they get it right, the Guesser takes their place and they become the new Guesser.

## Variations:

▶ Thread a little bell on the string to encourage really quiet passing.

# Obstacle course

**Group size:** any
**Age:** any
**Equipment:** mats, hoops,
ropes, tunnels, barrels,
tents, bean bags,
balancing bars,
balls, stepping stones,
buckets, boxes,
dressing-up clothes
and chalk

Obstacle courses are great fun. You can make them with any sort of equipment and they can be as challenging as you like. For younger children, make the challenges simple and keep the height of equipment low, so there is no risk of falling. You can even make a challenge using just chalk and ropes.

## How to play:

1. Work with the children to construct the obstacle race. Younger children may need to have the concept explained to them, and may just need a couple of obstacles to start with.

2. Let the children explore the obstacles freely to start with.

3. When they have practiced each challenge, agree on starting and finishing points, and take turns to go round the obstacle race.

4. Older children can make the course into a race and play in teams.

## Variations:

▶ Add some hats, shoes or other dressing up clothes (but be careful that children can manage the challenges with the clothes on. Avoid trailing hems or sleeves, strings, ribbons etc).

▶ Use a stopwatch to time children as they do the challenges.

▶ Add new challenges as you or the children think of them. Be aware of risks and dangers, and always take into account both the age and the physical ability of the group you are working with.

# Put it on

**Group size:** an even number
**Age:** any
**Equipment:** dressing-up clothes (shoes, hats, coats, shirts, gloves and socks)

Running, hopping, skipping, jumping with dressing up clothes on is a new challenge and will cause much laughter and fun! For younger children, just have everybody in one team and do it for fun, or have lots of hats or shoes or shirts.

## How to play:

1. Divide the clothes into the number of heaps or baskets or boxes, so each team has a box with the same collection (e.g. a hat, shoes, shirt, scarf and gloves).

2. Get the children into two or more teams (this is a challenge for younger children, who need the teams to be small!).

3. Mark a line on the ground and put the boxes 10 or 20 metres away (the younger the children, the nearer the box needs to be).

4. When you say 'GO' the first member of the team runs from the starting line to the box, puts on all the clothes, runs back, takes off the clothes

5. The next player puts them on, runs to the box and takes them off, runs back and touches the next player, who runs and gets dressed.

6. The first team to finish wins.

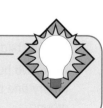

## Variations:

▶ Add extra clothes.
▶ Get them to hop, skip, jump instead of running.

# Bucket ball

**Group size:** three or four
**Age:** any
**Equipment:** bucket of balls for each group of children

Filling and emptying is a great way to use energy and have some fun at the same time. Ball pool balls, ping-pong balls, tennis balls are all suitable for this activity.

## How to play:

1. Put the balls in the bucket.
2. The children decide who will take balls out, and who will put them back.
3. When you say 'GO' one child takes balls out of the bucket one at a time and throws or rolls them away. The others have to retrieve them and put them back in the bucket.
4. Change the thrower when they get tired.

## Variations:

▶ Use bean bags for younger children, they don't go so far!

▶ Let the children bring back more than one ball at a time.

▶ Have two buckets (one empty and one full). See how long it takes to empty one bucket and fill the other. This variation is good for bigger groups.

# First hopscotch

**Group size:** any
**Age:** any
**Equipment:** playground
chalk, bean bags or
small stones

Preparation for playing hopscotch is very important. Firstly, very young children need to practice hopping or jumping along a number line marked on the floor or a carpet (you could use a piece of stair carpet outside, and paint the number line on it). Start with numbers from 1–5 and gradually increase the length of the line. Traditional Hopscotch needs tossing skills as well, so build these in as children's control develops.

## How to play:

**Here is a possible sequence of the development of Hopscotch skills:**

1. Walk along a number line of 1–5, counting as you go.

2. Walk along a number line of 1–5, turn round at the end and walk back, counting backwards.

3. Jump with feet together along the line and back.

4. Hop along the line and back.

5. Do steps 1 to 4 on a 1–10 number line.

6. Practice doing feet together jump, then hop, feet together jump, then hop, (not along the line!)

7. Do this along the 1–10 line and back, balancing on one leg as you turn round on 10.

8. Do some balancing on one leg practice.

9. Practice balancing on one leg and picking up a bean bag from the floor!

10. Practice tossing the bean bag in front of you, hopping over and picking it up.

Now they will be ready to play traditional Hopscotch!

# Traditional hopscotch

**Group size:** any
**Age:** when they are ready!
**Equipment:** playground chalk, bean bags or small stones

Mark out your hopscotch game on the playground or path. You could make a permanent game with playground paint, or make it on a carpet sample so you can roll it up when you are not using it.

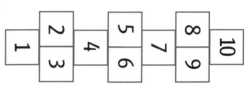

## How to play:

**Game 1:**

1. The first player hops onto the first square, jumps with feet apart onto 2 and 3, hops on 4, jumps with feet apart on 5 and 6, and so on to 10.

2. When they get to 10, they must turn round on one foot and return the same way.

**Game 2:**

1. The first player tosses their bean bag or stone on Square 1, jumps over it onto Squares 2 and 3, completes the Squares as in Game 1 till they get back to 2 and 3. Then they bend down, pick up their bean bag and jump over square 1 to get home.

2. All the players complete the Square 1 turn.

3. The first player then tosses their bean bag onto square 2, and so on till everyone has completed all 10 squares. This takes some time, so you may want to alter the rules for younger children!

## Variations:

▶ Play with each player taking all their turns at once as long as they don't wobble or miss-toss their bean bag.

▶ Draw a different game. Try a zigzag or spiral for hopping and jumping, or make a bigger hopscotch with more numbers.

# On your heads!

**Group size:** any
**Age:** any
**Equipment:** bean bags,
chalk and cones (optional)

Walking or running while balancing something on your head makes your brain work harder. It also helps with posture and general motor control. This activity combines fun with challenge, and is suitable for older as well as younger children.

## How to play:

1. Mark a starting line and a finishing line on the ground. Use your judgement about the distance apart, taking into account the age and experience of the children.

2. Players take turns to balance a bean bag on their head as they walk to the finishing line.

3. When they reach the finish, they can take the bean bag off and carry it as they run back and give it to the next player

4. Continue until everyone has had a go.

### Variations:

▶ Jump, hop or skip instead of running – or even walk backwards.

▶ Scatter some cones in a line, and get the children to zigzag round them.

▶ When everyone has had one go, go again with two bean bags.

▶ Use a quoit or a funny hat for a change.

# Fire on the mountain

**Group size:** you decide!
**Age:** any
**Equipment:** none

Fire on the Mountain is a game from Tanzania. It is best played on grass but can be played on the playground. There is no limit to the number of children that can play but you will know what the maximum is!

## How to play:

1. Start the game by choosing an adult or child as a leader.

2. Together, choose a 'signal word' – this could be a word or a name.

3. All the children find a space and lie on their backs with their eyes closed or covered with their hands. When they hear the special word, they must all jump up and onto their feet quickly.

4. The game begins with the leader shouting 'Fire on the mountain!'

5. All the players answer 'Fire!' but do not jump up.

6. The leader then shouts 'Fire on the...!'. Each time the leader changes the place where the fire may be, e.g. 'Fire on the elbow!', 'Fire on the knee!'. Other players repeat the words.

7. The leader chooses to shout the special word at any time – between or in the middle of a phrase – although it is better to get the idea of the game first and add the word at the end of the phrase.

8. When the leader says the special word, the player who jumps up last becomes the leader's helper and looks to see who jumps up last next time. The winner is the last player left in the game. You could allow a number of winners, who receive a round of applause.

The winners should also applaud everyone else for a good game.

# Negezza

**Group size:** 2–6
**Age:** older
**Equipment:** bean bags and chalk

Neggeza is a game from Libya. It's a bit like Hopscotch and you can use a 1–10 hopscotch grid or the one here.

## How to play:

1. Draw the grid with chalk and give each player a bean bag.
2. The first player hops on one foot and pushes their bean bag, using their hand, into Square 1.
3. They continue through the squares in number order.
4. The player keeps going unless the bean bag or their foot lands in the wrong square.
5. The next player takes over and tries to get all the way to Square 8.

| 7 | 8 |
|---|---|
|   | 6 |
| 4 | 5 |
| 3 |   |
| 2 |   |
| 1 |   |

**A much harder variation:**

If a player reaches Square 8 without making a mistake, they stand with their back to the grid and throw the bean bag over their shoulder. If it lands on a square, they or the adult supervising can write their name in the square. This is now their square and no one else may touch it with either their bean bag or their foot. Continue to play in turn and try to move up the board. With each player and as more squares are 'named', the game becomes harder. When it is impossible for anyone to play, the player with the most squares named is the winner.

# Sick cat (Gato duente)

**Group size:** at least six, not more than 30
**Age:** any
**Equipment:** cones/markers

Sick cat (Gato duente) is a game from Brazil. It needs a big space with edges defined by markers. It is a great summer game played outside in the sunshine. It is also very energetic, so have plenty of cooling off time and lots of water to drink in the shade!

## How to play:

1. One child is chosen to be the gato or cat. The other children spread themselves out in the defined space.

2. At a given signal the gato chases the others. Each player they touch becomes a gato duente or sick cat and must hold their hand over the part of the body touched by the gato.

3. The sick cats then join the gato in chasing the other players who become sick cats when they are touched too.

4. The winner/s is/are the player/s left untouched by the end of the game.

## Variations:

▶ Add a doctor who can make the sick cats well again by touching them so they can run again. Change the cat and the doctor regularly.

▶ Have a safe place (maybe inside a hoop or rope) where children can rest from the game for a while.

# Who is it?

**Group size:** from 6–10
**Age:** any
**Equipment:** none

good for practising
asking and answering
questions.

## How to play:

1.  Those who want to play form a line one behind the other. The person at the head of the line is 'IT' and must stand with their back to the other children.

2.  'IT' begins the game by asking questions:
    'Have you seen my friend?'
    OTHERS: 'No Sir/Madam.'
    'Do you know where s/he is?
    OTHERS: 'Yes Sir/Madam.'

3.  'IT' takes nine slow steps forward while the other children quickly change places behind them.

4.  One of the children stands immediately behind 'IT'.

5.  The others call out 'Who is it?'

6.  'IT' can ask three questions before guessing who is behind them – e.g. 'Is it a boy or girl?', 'Have they got dark or fair hair?', 'Are they small or tall?'

7.  The other players give one-word answers.

8.  After three questions, 'IT' must guess who is behind them. If they are right, they have another turn at 'IT'. If they are wrong, the child behind them becomes 'IT' and the game begins again.

## Variations:

▶   Older children might enjoy playing this game with 'IT' wearing a scarf as a blindfold.

# Gee

**Group size:** 2 small teams
**Age:** older or more mature children
**Equipment:** none

Gee is a chasing game from England and it's perfect for playing outside. Some of you may recognise it as 40/40.

## How to play:

1. Make two small teams and decide which team will be hiders and which will be seekers.

2. Agree a starting place – a bench, tree, door etc.

3. The hiders go off and hide while the seekers close/cover their eyes and count to 20, 50 or 100 (you choose which)

4. The seekers then go in search of the hiders. When one of the seekers spots one of the hiders they shout 'GEE!'

5. All the seekers then run to the starting place and the hider who has been seen chases them.

6. If the seekers get back to the starting place without being caught, the hider becomes their prisoner.

7. But if the hider manages to touch one or more of the seekers before they reach the starting place, then all caught hiders are freed.

8. The hiders then run off and hide again.

9. The teams swap over when all the hiders have been caught.

# Look up, look down

**Group size:** 4 or more
**Age:** any
**Equipment:** none

This game should be played on grass as it involves sitting down very quickly and benefits from a soft landing! It is very good for encouraging young children to make eye contact with each other.

## How to play:

1. The children make a circle and are told to 'Look down'. While they are doing this, the leader tells them that when they are given the instruction to 'Look up' they must find someone to look at and who looks at them.

2. When they do this, they must both sit down as quickly as they can.

3. The fun comes as the remaining children look around, desperately trying to find a partner.

4. Repeat the game but, this time, tell the children that they must look at someone new. It is also worth reminding them not to agree who they are going to look at before they look down!

## Variations:

▶ Stand in a circle and do step 1. Then children must change places instead of sitting down.

# What are you doing?

**Group size:** 6–10
**Age:** 5+
**Equipment:** none

This is a lovely game for using imagination. Even the youngest children will amaze you with their ability to invent new and creative mimes! The minimum number for this game is about six while the maximum should be no more than fourteen.

## How to play:

1. The children make a circle and one is chosen to start the game. They stand in the middle of the circle and begin an action – jogging, reading a book, etc.

2. The other children in the circle say together 'What are you doing?'

3. The child in the middle must then say something other than what they are doing – for example, 'I'm eating an apple'.

4. The next in the circle stands up and does the new action as they come into the circle.

5. The children all say 'What are you doing?' and this child must invent another new activity – riding a bike, perhaps.

6. This continues until all the children have had a go. Once they have got used to the idea, they will begin to come up with some really wacky ideas for each other to act out – feeding chips to an elephant was a particularly memorable one!

## Variations:

▶ Younger children could just do the action and the person who guesses what they are doing has the next go.

# Zip, bop, zap

**Group size:** any
**Age:** any
**Equipment:** none

Clapping games that involve listening are good for making their brains work. Here is one that has many different names, but this is the one we like best!

## How to play:

1. The children make a circle and the leader introduces the first instruction – 'ZIP!' – This is a clap to the side while saying the word. The person next to the leader turns and repeats the movement and the word to the person next to them and so on around the circle.

1. Send this movement and word round the circle until they are familiar with it.

1. Now introduce 'BOP!' – Anyone can 'BOP!'. A 'BOP!' stops the 'ZIP!' and sends it back in the opposite direction. Everyone gets one chance to 'BOP!' (otherwise you have a fight over who can 'BOP!' the most in one part of the circle and the rest are left out!)

1. Start the 'ZIP!' again and see what happens when children start to 'BOP!' .

1. When the children are used to 'ZIP!' and 'BOP!' you can introduce 'ZAP!' – This sends the 'ZIP!' across the circle to the person you are looking at. Again only allow one 'ZAP!' each.

1. The game can continue until everyone has had their 'BOP!' and 'ZAP!', and it is just the 'ZIP!' being passed around the circle.

   * Use 'ROUND', 'BACK', and 'ACROSS' for younger children.

# Sausages

**Group size:** up to 20
**Age:** 5+
**Equipment:** none

The ideal number for this game is between ten and twenty. Again it is another circle game that allows for lots of fun in an easily controlled format.

## How to play:

1. Everyone stands or sits in a circle and one person is chosen to stand in the middle.

2. The children in the circle take it in turns to ask questions of the player in the middle.

3. The questions should be the 'What or where?' kind – for example, 'What do you brush your hair with?' or 'Where do you live?'

4. The player in the middle must always answer 'Sausages' (or another single word) without laughing, an almost impossible task with this age group!

5. If (more like when!) they laugh, they must change places with the child whose question brought on the giggles and the game begins again.

## Variations:

▶ Try this game with expressions. The children in the circle make silly faces and the one in the middle must try not to laugh. Or you could try silly noises!

# Statue laugh

**Group size:** up to 12
**Age:** any
**Equipment:** none

Another game of self control, Statue laugh can be played with between eight and twelve players.

## How to play:

1. Everyone stands in a circle and one person is chosen to stand in the middle.

2. The child in the middle gives the other children instructions – 'hop', 'stick your tongue out', 'put your fingers in your ears', etc.

3. At some point in the game, they call out 'STOP!' and all the other players must 'freeze' in the last position they took up.

4. The child in the middle then tries to make the others laugh by walking among them, pulling faces, making jokes or noises, etc. Emphasise that this child is not allowed to touch anyone.

5. The first person who does laugh becomes 'IT' and takes their place in the middle for the next round.

## Variations:

▶ Play 'Pop Stars' – the children dance to pop music and 'freeze' when the music stops. The first to move is out. Start the music again and dance or sing until the music stops again. The last one to be out dances and sings for everyone else, to enthusiastic applause!

# Animal statues

**Group size**: any
**Age**: any
**Equipment**: a tambourine
or drum

Imitating animals is fun and gets rid of a lot of energy! Try this version of a statue game to practice some animal movements.

## How to play:

1. Each child should stand in a space.
2. The leader calls out an animal name and the children move like that animal. Start with familiar ones!
3. When the drum or tambourine sounds, the children must freeze in their animal shapes until the leader calls another animal name.
4. Anyone who wobbles is out and stands with the leader to spot other 'wobblers'.
5. Continue until there are just a few children left.

## Variations:

▶ Play the game again. The first 'wobbler' stands near the leader and calls out the next animal name.

▶ Use other movements – try being different people – old ladies, babies, pop stars, dancers, teachers etc.

▶ Hold up animal pictures to encourage good looking.

# Giants, dwarves and wizards

**Group size:** two teams
**Age:** 5+
**Equipment:** none

This is a popular variation of Paper, Scissors, Stone. It can be played with a whole group split in half, but always benefits from having two adults supervise: one for each team.

## How to play:

1. Establish a 'home' - perhaps a chalk circle for each team.

2. Now, in secret, teams decide with their helper what character each of them is going to be – giants stand on tiptoe with their arms above their heads –dwarves crouch down low – wizards stand and wiggle their fingers out in front of them as if casting a spell.

3. Once everyone on each team has chosen what to be, they line up and face each other.

4. On the count of three, each person shows what they are.

5. Now everyone begins to chase or run to catch the right character. Giants capture dwarves, dwarves capture wizards, and wizards capture giants.

6. Anyone caught before they reach the agreed 'home' must join the other team.

## Variations:

▶ Each team decides what the whole team will be. They show their action and, following the rule, points can be awarded for the winning team. This variation works better with younger children as there is no temptation to change characters!

# Keeper of the treasure

**Group size:** any
**Age:** any
**Equipment:** a scarf or big hat, a chair, bells or tambourine for the 'treasure'

This is a game for children wanting a quieter activity filled with suspense! Don't be put off by the need for quiet in a busy area. The children's sense of hearing improves dramatically when this game is played!

## How to play:

1. Sit in a circle with the chair in the middle. Put the 'treasure' near the chair.

2. Choose one child to be the 'keeper'. They sit on the chair with the scarf or hat covering their eyes. If the child is not happy to do this, ask them to close their eyes or cover them with their hands.

3. Choose another child to sneak up to the treasure, take it and return to their place without the keeper hearing the noise of the treasure as it is moved.

4. If the keeper hears and points in the general direction of the 'creeper', then the treasure must be returned and another child is chosen to try and steal it away.

5. If the 'creeper' is successful and gets back to their place unheard, then they replace the keeper in the next round.

## Variations:

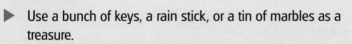

▶ Use a bunch of keys, a rain stick, or a tin of marbles as a treasure.

▶ Put a bunch of keys and a tin by the chair. The 'creeper' must put the keys in the tin and take them away without a sound.

# Fill the Bucket!

**Group size:** any
**Age:** any
**Equipment:** a bucket of water, an empty bucket, disposable paper or plastic cups

This is a game for a hot day, and it needs to be played outside. Have some towels ready for mopping up, and get your spare clothes box out!

## How to play:

**Game 1**

1. Put the full bucket at one end of the grass and the empty one at the other.
2. Give each child a cup and see how quickly they can transport the water from the full bucket to the empty one.

**Game 2**

1. Now make a couple of small holes half way up in each cup with a sharp pencil.
2. Play the game again with the leaky cups.

**Game 3**

Have two full buckets and two empty ones and have some simple races with whole and leaky cups.

**Game 4**

Play the same game with two clean dustbins for an even bigger splash!

# Do a dodge

**Group size:** 8–15
**Age:** any
**Equipment:** small sponge
balls, chalk

When you play this game, make sure that the children understand the rules.
The game is about touching the person with the ball, not hurting them, and the
balls must be aimed at legs, not faces.

## How to play:

1. Draw a circle for the children to stand in.
2. Two or three people stand in the middle of the circle.
3. The other children stand around the chalk circle. They have a sponge ball each.
4. These children aim the balls at the legs of the children in the middle. The children in the middle must dodge the balls as they come.
5. If one of the children is hit by a ball, they change places with the child who aimed it.

## Variations:

▶ Play the same game with rolling balls instead of throwing
– this makes it a much more controlled experience!

# Tails

**Group size:** up to 16
**Age:** any
**Equipment:** markers or cones, string, ribbon or wool, cut in lengths of about 50cm

The aim of this game is to develop chasing and dodging skills. It works best with a group of about sixteen children and needs a clearly defined playing space. (It's great fun for all ages!)

## How to play:

1. Give each child a piece of string to tuck into the back of one of their shoes. It should trail out behind them.

2. On 'GO!' they run around in the space and try to tread on other player's tails and pull them out of their owner's shoes. At the same time they try not to lose their own!

3. Lost tails must be picked up quickly and taken to the side where they can be re-attached. Then it's back into the game!

## Variations:

▶ Tuck the tails in waistbands, as illustrated.

# Pass the bean bag

**Group size:** up to 16
**Age:** any
**Equipment:** a bean bag

Pass the bean bag is a good game for emphasising co-operation. You can play this with a maximum of sixteen children, indeed, the more the merrier as this makes it harder for the child in the middle!

## How to play:

1. The children can either sit or stand in a circle with their hands behind their backs. The children need to be as close together as possible.

2. Choose one child to stand in the middle of the circle with their eyes closed/covered.

3. Give the bean bag to one child, who goes around the outside of the circle and places the bean bag in the hands of another child.

4. They then return to their place in the circle and the child in the middle opens/uncovers their eyes. They have three guesses to discover who has the bean bag.

5. The other children must try to pass the bean bag around behind their backs without the player in the middle spotting it moving!

## Variations:

▶ Make the game more difficult by using a bunch of keys or some bells!

# Spin the bottle

**Group size:** 6–10
**Age:** any
**Equipment:**
a plastic bottle,
securely sealed and
with some sand or
gravel inside for
weight

You can set this game up for between six and ten children. It needs a smooth surface.

## How to play:

1. The children stand in a circle and each one has a number. You could give them a number card or chalk their number on the ground in front of them if they might forget it.

2. One person is chosen to stand in the middle and they spin the bottle.

3. This child then calls out a number and the player with that number has to run into the middle and pick the bottle up before it stops spinning.

4. This player calls another number and has a turn to spin the bottle.

## Variations:

▶ Play the game calling children's names rather than numbers.

▶ Write the numbers 0–10 on the ground in a circle. Spin the bottle and when it stops, the children must clap, jump, stamp, hop that number of times.

▶ Use the spinning bottle to choose a child from a circle to do a trick, sing a song, say a nursery rhyme, tell a joke.

# Cat and mouse

**Group size:** 12–16
**Age:** any
**Equipment:** none

Cat and Mouse is another circle game for between twelve and sixteen children, and it has many variations. As with any chase game, it is important to maintain constant supervision.

## How to play:

1. Stand in a circle and hold hands.
2. The leader chooses one child to be the cat – they stand outside the circle - and another to be the mouse – they stand inside the circle.
3. The cat then tries to catch the mouse by getting in and out of the circle.
4. It is the job of the children forming the circle to try and allow the mouse to escape from the cat by lifting up their arms as the mouse scurries around.
5. If this is too difficult for the cat, introduce a count of seven with everyone's arms in the air. This gives the cat a better chance of catching the mouse.
6. Try to keep the game moving. Make sure that the players forming the circle do not crouch or bend down. Remember it is only their arms that can move up or down.

# One knee, two knees

Group size: any
Age: 5+
Equipment: a large
or small soft ball

A circle game that allows for a large number of children to play. It is easily made more challenging depending on the age and skill of the players.

## How to play:

1. Make a circle standing up, with a space between each of the children.

2. Choose one child to start. They must throw the ball to the player next to them.

3. If the player catches the ball then it is their turn to throw it to the next person and so on around the circle.

4. If the player drops the ball, they must kneel down on one knee before throwing it to the next person. They can be restored to standing if they successfully catch the next throw to them.

5. Further missed catches result in the player kneeling down on two knees, followed by only having one hand to catch, etc.

6. It is probably best to limit it to one hand as catching with laps may be a little too difficult for the very young!

## Variations:

▶ Play can move round the circle, or you may want to make it more difficult by allowing it to pass across the circle. You will be heartened by the many attempts that children will make to restore friends to standing again!

48

# Sharks

**Group size:** any
**Age:** any
**Equipment:** string or skipping ropes

This is a game of co-operation, not competition. The aim is to keep everyone safe, not capture the island!

## How to play:

1.  Make several 'islands' by tying string or ropes together to make circles.

2.  Scatter the circles around the playing area.

3.  The children choose an island to start from.

4.  The leader calls – 'SWIM' and everyone leaves their island to swim in the ocean round them.

5.  The leader or a helper removes one island.

6.  When the leader shouts 'SHARKS!' everyone runs to get on an island. As the islands are removed, the children will have to work harder to rescue everyone and keep them on the island.

## Variations:

▶ Have more than one word to shout. For instance 'DIVE' could mean hold your head under the water; 'WHIRLPOOL' could mean spin round and round.

▶ For older children, you could shout a number of people who can get onto one island – make sure the numbers of players and islands work, or some people will be left to the sharks!

# Make a snake

**Group size:** any
**Age:** younger children
**Equipment:** none

Make a snake is best played indoors or on grass, as it involves rolling and sliding on the ground! It's most suitable for younger players, but Reception children will enjoy some of the variations.

## How to play:

1. Lie down in twos, one holding the other's ankles.
2. Now move like a snake, without letting go!
3. Now see if one snake can join with another to make a four person snake – can it move around?
4. As children get used to the game, can they make snakes of eight? or more? or the whole group?
5. Can the snakes go through a tunnel? Can they go under a blanket? Can they go over the mountains (a cushion)?

## Variations:

▶ Make a standing up snake, with children holding each other's waists. What can this snake do?

▶ How about a snake of children touching but not holding hands. Can this snake stay together?

# All change

**Group size:** 6–20
**Age:** any
**Equipment:** a chair for each child

In this classic circle game, players must listen carefully, and look at each other so they don't bump or lose their chair!

## How to play:

**Game 1**

1. Everyone sits on a chair in a circle.
2. The leader calls 'All Change everyone wearing blue.' or 'All Change everyone with black hair.' or 'All Change everyone with a baby at home.'
3. Continue until everyone has had a go.

**Game 2**

1. Everyone sits on a chair in a circle.
2. One child stands in the circle and the chair is removed
3. The child calls an 'All Change' instruction which describes themselves as well as other children.
4. They will get a seat and the child without a seat is the next caller.

# Girls and boys

**Group size:** any
**Age:** any
**Equipment:** a parachute

Parachute games are a useful standby for spare moments, but they are also very valuable for building co-operation and collaboration. If you haven't got a parachute, use a big piece of lightweight fabric.

## How to play:

1. The children make a circle and you decide whether they need to sit or stand.

2. Everyone holds the edge of the parachute and stands still until you give the following instruction:

    'All the boys!' – This means that all the girls and the adults hold the parachute up above their heads while the leader counts 1-2-3.

3. During this time, the boys in the group cross underneath the parachute and try to get to the other side before the end of the count when the parachute is brought back down.

4. Give other instructions such as:
    'All the girls!'
    The names of two children to change places across the circle.
    Children with names beginning with a chosen letter.
    Children with pets/brothers/sisters/blue eyes, etc.

See The Little Book of Parachute Play for more ideas.

# Colour ball

**Group size:** any
**Age:** any
**Equipment:** a large, soft ball and a parachute

Another parachute game to try. This one really improves concentration and co-operation!

## How to play:

1. Begin with all the children holding the parachute still and flat on the floor.
2. Place the ball in the middle of the parachute.
3. Explain that the children have to work together to get the ball to stop on the colour you call out.
4. Say the colour that they are aiming for.
5. Give the instruction 'GO!' and encourage the group to work together in making the ball reach its target.

## Variations:

▶ Tell the children that the aim of the game is to make the ball reach a certain child in the group. When this is achieved, this child decides who should be the next person to receive the ball.

▶ Try the same game with a teddy or other soft toy

# Bear hugs

**Group size:** any
**Age:** any
**Equipment:** none

This game gets children to empathise with each other, see similarities and show affection. It is just as good for older children as it is for nursery age.

## How to play:

1. Children spread themselves out in a reasonable space.
2. The leader calls an instruction such as 'Everyone who is four, hug each other', or 'Everyone with fair hair, hug each other', or 'Everyone wearing red, hug each other' or 'Everyone who likes bananas, hug each other'
3. All the children the instruction applies to must get together in a group hug.

## Variations:

▶ Children walk around in the space until they get a 'shake hands' or 'wave' instruction. If the instruction does not apply to them they continue to walk, if it does, they find someone who has that feature and shake hands with them or wave to them.

▶ Put a coloured square of card in four different places on the ground. Weight them down with a stone if you need to. The children walk around till the leader calls out a colour. Children wearing that colour run to the right square. Others keep walking.

# Sleeping lions

**Group size:** any
**Age:** any
**Equipment:** a large, soft ball

This is a very old game – sometimes called 'Dead Lions' and is a very good game for the end of a lively session when you want the children to calm down and relax. The only problem is some may fall asleep, especially children who have been used to an afternoon nap!

## How to play:

1. Children choose a space and lie down in a comfortable position. They pretend to be asleep.

2. Any child who moves joins the leader and helps to watch the remaining sleeping lions.

## Variations:

► Play 'Roosting Birds', standing on one leg for as long as they can.

► Play 'Sleeping Horses' standing up.

# Call a colour

**Group size:** any
**Age:** any
**Equipment:** chalk

Not all races have to be fast!
Slow, walking, stepping and
balancing races are all good
fun, and they help to develop
physical control of muscles
and limbs.

## How to play:

1. All the children start on a chalk line.
2. The leader (adult or child) calls out a colour.
3. Children wearing that colour take two steps forward. Others stay put.
4. Carry on calling colours until someone reaches the finishing line.

## Variations:

▶ Have a slow bike race with trikes and bikes. The slowest
  player wins, but they mustn't put their feet down.

▶ Have a backwards walking race – when children can manage it!

▶ Have a fast walking race. Children soon get the idea of fast walking and
  the difference between this and running!

# Mirror me

**Group size:** any
**Age:** any
**Equipment:** none

Copying games are another traditional group. They help children to concentrate, look carefully and control their bodies, isolating different parts and locating left and right sides.

## How to play:

**Game 1**

1.  Children sit or stand in a semi-circle.

2.  One child or an adult stands in front of the group and 'strikes a pose' for example, one arm raised and the other behind their back.

3.  Everyone else copies the movement.

**Game 2**

1.  Children choose a partner.

2.  One child makes a single movement for their friend to copy.

3.  Develop this by making a short series of movements.

**Game 3 (children love this version!)**

1.  Play a listening version. This is also a very good game for learning body parts.

2.  Give two instructions such as 'Put your hand on your head and your foot on your knee.' 'Put your finger on your elbow and your chin on your shoulder.' 'Put your forehead on your knee and your hand on your head.'

3.  Make the game harder by giving three instructions.

# Here we go round

**Group size:** any
**Age:** any
**Equipment:** none

### Here we Go Round the Mulberry Bush

## How to play:

1. Children stand in a ring to do the actions, walk or skip round to the chorus.

   Here we go round the mulberry bush,
   The mulberry bush, the mulberry bush,
   Here we go round the mulberry bush,
   On a cold and frosty morning.

(Stop and follow the action)

   This is the way we clean our teeth,
   Clean our teeth, clean our teeth,
   This is the way we clean our teeth,
   On a cold and frosty morning.

(Repeat the chorus and follow with another action such as:)

   This is the way we comb our hair
   This is the way we wash our hands
   This is the way we eat some toast etc.

## Variations:

▶ Sing other words such as 'Here we go round with all our friends', or 'These are the things we do at school.' Add movements such as 'This is the way we paint a picture...' 'This is the way we build with bricks....' etc.

# This old man

**Group size:** any
**Age:** any
**Equipment:** none

## This Old Man

## How to play:

1. Children stand in a ring to do the actions.

**A.** This old man, he played one,
He played nicknack on my drum,
With a nicknack paddywack
Give a dog a bone
This old man came rolling home

**B.** This old man, he played two,
He played nicknack on my shoe,
With a nicknack etc.

**C.** This old man, he played three,
He played nicknack on my knee,
With a nicknack etc.

**D.** This old man, he played four,
He played nicknack on my door,
With a nicknack etc.

**E.** This old man, he played five,
He played nicknack on my hive,
With a nicknack etc.

**F.** This old man, he played six,
He played nicknack on my sticks,
With a nicknack etc.

**G.** This old man, he played seven,
He played nicknack down in Devon,
With a nicknack etc.

**H.** This old man, he played eight,
He played nicknack on my gate,
With a nicknack etc.

**I.** This old man, he played nine,
He played nicknack on my line,
With a nicknack etc.

**J.** This old man, he played ten,
He played nicknack on my hen,
With a nicknack, etc.

# The wheels on the bus

**Group size:** any
**Age:** any
**Equipment:** none

## The Wheels on the Bus

## How to play:

This song is best played in a circle

> The wheels on the bus go round and round,
> round and round, round and round.
> The wheels on the bus go round and round,
> All day long

(roll hands like wheels)

> The wipers on the bus go swish, swish, swish,
> Swish, swish, swish,swish, swish, swish.
> The wipers on the bus go swish, swish, swish,
> All day long

(swish hands like wipers)

Continue with

> The lights on the bus go flash, flash, flash
> The babies on the bus go 'Waa, waa, waa....'
> The mums on the bus go chat, chat, chat
> The grandads on the bus go nod, nod, nod
> The girls/boys on the bus go 'Giggle, giggle, giggle......'
> The driver on the bus goes 'Tickets please,' 'Tickets please,' 'Tickets please.'

# Wind the bobbin

**Group size:** any
**Age:** any
**Equipment:** none

## Wind the Bobbin

## How to play:

This song is best played in a circle

> Wind the bobbin up, wind the bobbin up,

(winding motion with hands)

> Pull, pull, clap, clap, clap.

(follow words)

> Wind it back again, wind it back again.

(winding motion in other direction)

> Pull, pull, clap, clap, clap.

(follow words)

> Point to the ceiling, point to the floor
> Point to the window, point to the door,
> Clap your hands together, one, two, three,
> Put your hands upon your knees.

# In and out the dusty bluebells

**Group size:** any
**Age:** any
**Equipment:** none

## How to play:

1.  The children stand with their hands joined and raised to form a circle of arches.
2.  One child then goes in and out of the arches while others sing the song.
3.  On 'Tippety, tappety', the child stops behind the nearest one in the ring and taps gently on their shoulder.
4.  The chosen child joins behind the first one and they continue for another verse.
5.  Repeat the song until only one arch is left and the line is very long.

### In and Out the Dusty Bluebells

In and out the dusty bluebells,
In and out the dusty bluebells,
In and out the dusty bluebells,
Will you be my partner?
Tippety, tappety on your shoulder
Tippety, tappety on your shoulder
Tippety, tappety on your shoulder
Come and be my partner.

# Oranges and lemons

**Group size:** any
**Age:** any
**Equipment:** none

## How to play:

1. Two children join hands to make an arch. One is 'orange', one is 'lemon'.

2. The other children join in a line, hands on each others' waists.

3. They sing the song as they walk through the arch, round and through again.

4. When they get to the last line of the song (whichever one you choose!) the two 'arch' children bring down their arms to capture one child.

5. This child chooses 'orange' or 'lemon' and stands behind the chosen child in the arch.

6. Repeat the song until all the children have been caught.

### Oranges and Lemons

'Oranges and lemons,' say the bells of Saint Clement's,
'I owe you five farthings,' say the bells of Saint Martin's,
'When will you pay me?' say the bells of Old Bailey,
'When I grow rich,' say the bells of Shoreditch,
'When will that be,' say the bells of Stepney,
'I do not know,' says the great bell of Bow.
Here come a candle to light you to bed,
And here comes a chopper to chop off your head!

**an alternative might be:**

And here comes your mother to tuck you in bed.

# If you're happy

**Group size:** any
**Age:** any
**Equipment:** none

## If You're Happy and You Know It

## How to play:

**1.** Stand in a group and follow the movements as you sing.

If you're happy and you know it clap your hands, (clap, clap)
If you're happy and you know it clap your hands, (clap, clap)
If you're happy and you know it and you really want to show it,
If you're happy and you know it clap your hands, (clap, clap)

Verse 2

If you're happy and you know it stamp your feet, (stamp, stamp)

Verse 3

If you're happy and you know it wiggle your nose, (wiggle, wiggle)

Verse 4

If you're happy and you know it wave your arms, (wave, wave)

Verse 5

If you're happy and you know it do all four, (clap, clap, stamp, stamp, wiggle, wiggle, wave, wave)

Continue with variations and children's ideas.

# One finger, one thumb

**Group size:** any
**Age:** any
**Equipment:** none

## One Finger, One Thumb

## How to play:

**Verse 1** One finger, one thumb keep moving,
One finger, one thumb keep moving,
One finger, one thumb keep moving,
We'll all be merry and bright.

**Verse 2** One finger, one thumb, one arm, one leg keep moving,
One finger, one thumb, one arm, one leg keep moving,
One finger, one thumb, one arm, one leg keep moving,
We'll all be merry and bright.

**Verse 3** One finger, one thumb, one arm, one leg, one nod of the head,
keep moving, etc.

**Verse 4** One finger, one thumb, one arm, one leg, one nod of the head,
stand up, sit down, keep moving etc

**Verse 5** One finger, one thumb, one arm, one leg, one nod of the head,
stand up, turn round, sit down, keep moving etc.

**Verse 6** One finger, one thumb, one arm, one leg, one nod of the head,
stand up, turn round, sit down, roll over, keep moving etc.

**Verse 7** One finger, one thumb, one arm, one leg, one nod of the head,
stand up, turn round, sit down, roll over, clap hands, keep moving etc.

This could go on for ever!

# The okey cokey

**Group size**: any
**Age**: any
**Equipment**: none

## The Okey Kokey

## How to play:

1. Stand in a circle while you sing.
   Follow the words, putting the right part of your body in the circle as you sing.
   For the okey kokey, join your hands and rock left and right, then turn around.
   When you get to the whole self verse, jump in and out of the circle.

Verse 1  Put your right arm in, put your right arm out,
         In, out, in, out, and shake it all about.
         Do the okey kokey and turn around;
         That's what it's all about.

Chorus  Oh, okey kokey kokey, oh, okey kokey kokey,
        Oh, okey kokey kokey, knees bend, arms stretch, ra ra ra

Verse 2  Put your left arm in, left arm out etc.

Verse 3  Put your right leg in, right leg out etc.

Verse 4  Put your left leg in, left leg out etc.

Verse 5  Put your whole self in, your whole self out etc.

## Variations:

▶ You could add other parts of the body to the song, such as
  hands, head, shoulders, knees, elbows, ankles and ears.

# The princess

**Group size:** any
**Age:** any
**Equipment:** none

**There Was a Princess Long Ago**

## How to play:

1. Stand in a ring with one child in the middle as the princess and two others ready selected to play the wicked fairy and the prince

**Verse 1** There was princess long ago, long ago, long ago,
There was princess long ago, long ago, long ago,

The princess stands in the middle of the ring.

**Verse 2** And she lived in a big high tower etc.
Children raise hands to form arches

**Verse 3** A wicked fairy waved her wand etc.
Fairy waves wand at princess

**Verse 4** The princess slept for a hundred years etc.
Princess sleeps

**Verse 5** A big tall forest grew around etc.
Raise and join arms for trees

**Verse 6** A handsome prince came riding by etc.
Prince gallops round outside the ring

**Verse 7** He took his sword and chopped it down etc.
Prince gently 'chops' the arms of the 'forest'

**Verse 8** He took her hand to wake her up etc.
Prince takes her hand

**Verse 9** So everybody's happy now etc.
Everyone dances in pairs

# The big ship sails

**Group size:** any
**Age:** any
**Equipment:** none

## The Big Ship Sails

## How to play:

1. Children join hands in a long line.
1. The child at one end of the line puts their hand up against a wall to make an arch. The leader at the other end leads the children through the arch until the last child is through – the wall end child now has his/her arms crossed. The leader then goes through the next gap between the first child and the second, and so on until all the children have their arms crossed. Repeat the Verse 1 only until this point.

### Verse 1
The big ship sails on the Alley Alley O;
The Alley Alley O; the Alley Alley O;
The big ship sails on the Alley Alley O;
On the last day of September.

### Verse 2
The captain said, 'It will never, never do,
Never, never do; never, never do,'
The captain said, 'It will never, never do',
On the last day of September.

### Verse 3
The big ship sank to the bottom
of the sea,
The bottom of the sea, the bottom
of the sea,
The big ship sank to the bottom
of the sea,
On the last day of September.

### Verse 4
We all dip our heads in the deep
blue sea,
The deep blue sea, the deep
blue sea,
We all dip our heads in the deep
blue sea,
On the last day of September.

# Sandy girl

**Group size:** any
**Age:** any
**Equipment:** none

## Sandy Girl

## How to play:

1. Make a circle, sitting down.
2. One child sits in the middle of the circle, head in hands, sad and lonely.
3. The others get up and walk round in a circle, singing the song.
4. The child in the middle then chooses a friend to join them in the middle. They hold hands and skip around while others clap and la,la the song again.

There's a little sandy girl/sandy boy,
Sitting on a stone;
Crying, crying, because she's all alone.
Rise up little sandy girl/sandy boy,
Dry your tears away!
Choose the one you love the best
To come out to play.

5. The chosen friend sits in the middle for the next turn.

# Some other ideas for outdoor activities and games

While this book has concentrated mainly on games that can be played in large groups and in circles, there are other games and activities that work very well for those children who may not wish to be part of a large group. Marbles, French skipping, jacks, cats cradle, and many others are all excellent traditional games that require little space and still encourage involvement from even the youngest or most reticent child.

## Fundraising

Of course, all of these games require equipment and cost money. However, there is help at hand! By using this book as a starting point for discussion amongst colleagues and parents, you could organise an event where games of all kinds are celebrated. Parents, carers and families should be encouraged to sponsor their children to take part in as many of these games as possible. Indeed, they should be asked to come and see what your setting is trying to achieve by raising awareness of the value of games and game playing from a young age.

Of course, parents can add to your stock of games by remembering favourites from their childhood. This could have the added benefit of adding some of their own experience of games from their childhood.

Regional variations will provide a fascinating comparison as well as improving the game playing repertoire of your setting. With adults sharing their knowledge of games at shared events, and by teaching them to a new generation, they help to form a growing resource for the setting and the community.

Why not make a book of local games, with each one written by the person who contributed it, and accompanied by their photo?

# The Little Books Club

There is always something in Little Books to help and inspire you.
Packed full of lovely ideas, Little Books meet the need for exciting and
practical activities that are fun to do, address the Early Learning Goals
and can be followed in most settings. Everyone is a winner!

We publish 5 new Little Books a year. Little Books Club members receive
each of these 5 books as soon as they are published for a reduced price.
The subscription cost is £37.50 – a one off payment that buys
the 5 new books for £7.50 instead of £8.99 each.

In addition to this, Little Books Club Members receive:
· Free postage and packing on anything ordered from the
  Featherstone catalogue
· A 15% discount voucher upon joining which can be used to buy any
  number of books from the Featherstone catalogue
· Members price of £7.50 on any additional Little Book purchased
· A regular, free newsletter dealing with club news, special offers and
  aspects of Early Years curriculum and practice
· All new Little Books on approval - return in good condition within 30
  days and we'll refund the cost to your club account

Call 020 7440 2446 or email: littlebooks@acblack.com for
an enrolment pack. Or download an application form from our website:
## www.acblack.com/featherstone

# The **Little Books** series consists of:

| | | |
|---|---|---|
| All Through the Year | Listening | Sewing and Weaving |
| Bags, Boxes & Trays | Living Things | Small World Play |
| Bricks and Boxes | Look and Listen | Sound Ideas |
| Celebrations | Making Books and Cards | Storyboards |
| Christmas | Making Poetry | Storytelling |
| Circle Time | Mark Making | Seasons |
| Clay and Malleable Materials | Maths Activities | Time and Money |
| | Maths from Stories | Time and Place |
| Clothes and Fabrics | Maths Songs and Games | Treasure Baskets |
| Colour, Shape and Number | Messy Play | Treasureboxes |
| Cooking from Stories | Music | Tuff Spot Activities |
| Cooking Together | Nursery Rhymes | Washing Lines |
| Counting | Outdoor Play | Writing |
| Dance | Outside in All Weathers | |
| Dance, with music CD | Parachute Play | |
| Discovery Bottles | Persona Dolls | |
| Dough | Phonics | |
| 50 | Playground Games | |
| Fine Motor Skills | Prop Boxes for Role Play | |
| Fun on a Shoestring | Props for Writing | |
| Games with Sounds | Puppet Making | |
| Growing Things | Puppets in Stories | |
| ICT | Resistant Materials | |
| Investigations | Role Play | |
| Junk Music | Sand and Water | |
| Language Fun | Science through Art | |
| Light and Shadow | Scissor Skills | |

All available from

# www.acblack.com/featherstone